How to Win

After Loss

FLEDA BENNIE

How to Win After Loss

Author: **Fleda Bennie**

Copyright © 2020 by Fleda Bennie

ISBN – 9780578652207

Dedication

I want to thank so many people for helping me in this endeavor, though there are more than I can name. First, this book is dedicated to my wonderful, late husband Don, "DW," D Dubya, "Big Guy." I started this book long before he left this earth, but his love and strength helped me finish. He loved me deeply and truly and always thought I could do anything. He saw me as much more than I saw myself and changed me from a scared little girl to a woman who is able to walk on without him by my side.

Deep gratitude to my wonderful family. I have six incredible kids—three sons and three daughters-in-love who have given me the best grandchildren in the world: ten of them! These sixteen people are my strength, future, hope, joy, support, and much more. They have been with me through the loss of their own father and grandfather and then my bout with cancer. Their love is invaluable to me. There are not words to express my love for my family, and all of you understand that.

Thank you, Tami Gaupp, for being my "spark" to get me going; Dick and Donna Sorenson, life-long friends who have taught and inspired me more than they will ever know; and my dear friends at my church, Center Point—Pastors Allen & Sharon Yadon, their entire family, the staff, and really everyone there as they have supported, loved, encouraged, and stood with me as I passed through the Valley of the Shadow of Death.

To the ladies from Women on Wheels, your sacrifices for me through the past few years have inspired and humbled me. I hope to be able to pay forward your generosity and love for me.

I have friends at my business who sacrificed their time and life to help me maintain mine through Don's passing and then cancer. Again, I cannot begin to repay or match what you have done, but I want you to know that your love helped me stand and move forward. Especially my dear friend, Connie. I can never thank you enough for what you did for me in my darkest hours. You are amazing.

All praise goes to my God and Savior who is my life and breath, the One I love above all else. He has been my strength and shield, helping me to see beauty in the dark places. Forever and ever my praises will be raised to Him, my Light and Life.

Thanks to all who read my book. I don't pretend to know everything; I just know my own journey and hope it will be a help to someone else. I pray you find a word that helps you to cross the finish line and obtain the prize of the high calling in Jesus Christ.

"But whatever I used to count as my greatest accomplishments, I've written them off as a loss because of the Anointed One. I now realize that all I gained and thought was important was

nothing but yesterday's garbage compared to knowing the Anointed Jesus my Lord. For Him, I have thrown everything aside—it's nothing but a pile of waste—so that I may gain Him. When it counts, I want to be found belonging to Him, not clinging to my own righteousness based on law, but actively relying on the faithfulness of the Anointed One. This is true righteousness, supplied by God, acquired by faith. I want to know Him inside and out. I want to experience the power of His resurrection and join in His suffering, shaped by His death, so that I may arrive safely at the resurrection from the dead. I'm not there yet, nor have I become perfect; but I am charging on to gain anything and everything the Anointed One, Jesus, has in store for me—and nothing will stand in my way because He has grabbed me and won't let go. Brothers and sisters, as I said, I know I have not arrived; but there's one thing I am doing: I'm leaving my old life behind, putting everything on the line for this mission. I am sprinting toward the only goal that counts: to cross the line, to win the prize, and to hear God's call to resurrection life found exclusively in Jesus the Anointed." (Philippians 3:7-14, The Voice)

FLEDA BENNIE

Introduction

T hrough many years of ministry, I have had the opportunity to experience wonderful wins following epic loss. I have seen and known firsthand that the Christian realm does not deal with it easily—especially in any type of leadership position. I refer here to *spiritual loss*. Not just losing a battle, but losing vision, ministry, or position. Watching your dream and what you thought was God's dream for you die; being helpless to change the outcome or the hurt; being helpless to explain why.

We love the word and idea of a 'win.' Losing is a word that brings up visions of being a *loser*. To us there is no such thing as second place: you either win or lose, and only winners are remembered. Unfortunately, this same rule of living is applied to the spiritual kingdom and so the church contains defeated and offended Christians who hang their heads in shame or blame the devil or the pastor; who give up on ministry; who give up on other Christians; who may become hard and critical; who may become sad pretenders spending years of their life looking back at the past.

But the rules of earthly life do not apply to a spiritual kingdom. According to earthly standards, Christ Himself lost. When He came to earth, He did not successfully overthrow the Roman Empire and claim the throne of David; in fact, He was crucified. In the world's eyes, He lost, and the Empire won. But is He a "loser"?

I would hope that no one who is reading this would see Him in that way. He is the ultimate victor. He understood what it really meant to win! He is our example of how to be victorious in loss, of dealing with injustice at the hands of man, in watching the awful choices of humanity lead to hell, in enduring the loss of His own creation (us) because of injustice and terrible choices, and yet being the ultimate winner!

My husband and I served as ministers in both staff and lay positions for over 34 years: leading Bible Studies and worship, teaching Sunday School, and serving as elders in our church and pastors in our own church. We oversaw the Pastoral Department and served as business administrators and senior pastors. We were also on the leadership team in my church, and I continue in that capacity after my husband's death.

Ministry, whether full time or as a lay person, is never what we think it will be. It is far more wonderful and more desperately difficult than any of us imagined before we stepped into it. Its rewards are unlike any other, but its battles are more devious and surprising than we may have anticipated. And though we may have expected being wounded in a few skirmishes, none of us planned to lose a major battle!

This book is about winning after losing and doing it with dignity and in victory. That may sound impossible, but remember: in a kingdom where you have to die in order to live, you also have to lose in order to win!

Fleda Bennie

Contents

CHAPTER 1

About Me

"Do not yield to fear, for I am always near.
Never turn your gaze from me,[a] for I am
your faithful God I will infuse you with my
strength and help you in every situation.
I will hold you firmly with my victorious right
hand". Isaiah 41:10

I accepted Christ when I was nineteen years old. At that time, my husband was in Vietnam, I had a baby, and I was alone and afraid. One night, a Billy Graham crusade was on TV, and at the end of it I knelt down by myself and accepted Christ. I did the same thing the next two nights as well because I had no one to tell me whether or not it took the first time! My landlady was a Christian, so I talked with her. She helped me and invited me to church, and I have been in one ever since.

My husband came home from Vietnam to a Christian wife and a baby he did not know. A year later, he fell to his knees when a pastor—whom he didn't even like—stopped by for a visit. As he was leaving, the pastor turned and said, "Don, I think we need to pray because you need to accept Christ." I watched in stunned silence as my tough-guy husband fell to his knees crying and accepted Christ as his Savior.

Life did not immediately become a fairy tale—indeed we went through some very, very difficult times—but we loved each other, and the word *divorce* was not in our vocabulary.

A few years later, I was baptized in the Holy Spirit. Again, I was all alone praying and saw a sort of ticker tape running through my mind with words on it I didn't recognize. I spoke them out anyway. I did not know what had happened to me. I did not know about being baptized in the Spirit. I had been told that speaking in tongues was of the devil and had ended in the first century. I didn't tell anyone because I didn't know who to talk to about it.

I did know Don would think I had joined the devil, especially since we were experiencing a rough patch in our marriage, and our relationship had grown cold. But there was a woman at our church who was not like everyone else—very happy and outgoing—so I called her. She talked to me about what had happened and explained it to me. She said the same thing had happened to her and gave me a book to read more about the Holy Spirit. Apparently this was happening to lots of people, just not in my church.

I waited several months to tell my husband. As expected, the reaction was not good. He would not talk to me until we went to bed and turned out the lights; then he told me this was the devil. One day, I left that book, *The Holy Spirit and You*, on his chair. I didn't talk to him about it or nag him, I just loved him. One Saturday, he decided to take the book, "brush the dust off his Bible" (his words), go into the bedroom, and prove me wrong. Guess what? He came out and wanted to pray. And so, he too was baptized in the Spirit.

He later told me that he had considered leaving me because he thought I had lost my mind. However he saw a change in me, how happy I had become. He would come home from work and, to him, it seemed that I was floating on air. I was unaware of this, but it was God's way of showing him the truth and bringing us back together again as one. We stayed in our church and were asked to lead a home group, where everyone experienced the same thing.

Our church didn't believe in the Baptism of the Holy Spirit the way we were experiencing it, but it began happening regardless of that. The people in our home group asked us what was different about us, so we told them. They received the Baptism, and it changed them, too. We eventually moved to a different area and started attending a new church, where we ended up in leadership. From there, the years of being in leadership unfolded along with the joys and troubles that are a part of life.

As we changed and grew as Christians, my husband and I both felt the call to ministry. Over our lifetime of ministry, we experienced many kinds of joy, hurt, rejection, growth, laughter, tears, soaring hope, and crushing defeat. We experienced a great deal of loss. We also experienced much joy and fulfillment.

Over our lifetime in ministry, we experienced many kinds of joy, hurt, rejection, growth, laughter, tears, soaring hope and crushing defeat.

However, those are the easy parts to live with. We are human, and the losses often wiped out the victories because they were emotionally and spiritually overwhelming. From the time we were in our early 20's until we were in our mid 60s (yes, I'm old), we have been in ministry, whether in lay positions, on staff, as elders, or as senior pastors. We have experienced loss in every position. But we stayed with it; we survived. We learned from everything we went through, and we were victorious. We gained some scars, but we also grew so much in our relationship with our God that the losses became victories.

In 2015, I experienced the greatest loss of all: the death of my wonderful husband Don—my partner, my love, my best friend—in a motorcycle accident. I was with him riding my own bike, and he went to heaven instantly. This is not a story about losing my husband, but I will say I saw that, through all the loss we had experienced, God had already established things in my life that helped me through this greatest loss of all. My life here on earth is not the same, but I experience victories every day, and I rejoice that my dear Don is in heaven with Jesus, free of pain and sickness, rejoicing at the throne.

For many, many months, there was no rejoicing here on earth. There was grief, sadness, loneliness, fear, confusion, and the loss of every vision or dream I had, because all of them were wrapped around being two, not one. The pain of grief is the worst I have ever felt. The pain is physical, emotional, and spiritual. Today, hope and vision are returning, but it is a process that takes time, tears, prayer, trust, and thanksgiving.

In our lives, we started two churches that died miserably. We had bad experiences with senior pastors who used and abused us. We had ministries ripped out from under us. We were rejected like babies left in a basket on a doorstep. We lost friends who we thought had been our best friends. We cried. We agonized over what was wrong with us. We felt lost. We felt abandoned. We were angry. We tried to never go back to any church again. We were wounded and unable to function at times. But we never gave up. We never turned against God or abandoned the church. We took a while to heal, but we kept our eyes on Jesus.

In the end, we won!

I want you to know I am writing this from a perspective of having been through what you may be going through. I understand how you are feeling. Because I have gone through all of this, I also understand the (often justified) anger, betrayal, and hopelessness you may be feeling. You may be so overwhelmed with it that you long to just turn away. I hope that reading my story will help you know that these feelings are normal. They're the natural response to the kind of pain you've faced. Even though it feels that you are all alone, you are not. It may be hard to find those who can pour out the grace and healing love you need. I assure you, there are people out there, like me, who would happily do just that. They have grown fruit borne of pain and want to share it with you.

For my husband and I, we did our healing while remaining in the church. We believe strongly that the church belongs to Christ, not us—that though it may not look the way we think it should, God will change it. We had faith that God completes every work He begins: the church, the Bride of Christ is no exception. So taking Hosea as our model, who remained faithful to his unfaithful and faulty bride, we stayed. And God was faithful to heal us.

As followers of Christ, we know that ultimately He leads us through our pain into renewed love, to forgiveness—even and especially of the people who hurt us. Christ loved those who rejected Him, and we are called to be like Him. But this process cannot be rushed or forced, and there are no shortcuts. The only way out is through. In fact, if you try to rush it (or if well-meaning believers try to force you), it can make things worse. In the words of Christian author and speaker Mary DeMuth,

> *"Recovery takes years of stops and starts, and forgiveness is not a one-time easy decision, particularly if it's demanded or expected right away for the sake of peace and putting something shameful behind you. Often we see in*

communities of faith that victims are admonished to be grace-like, offering instant forgiveness to their abuser as if it could be doled out like a trinket or candy. And when someone is pressured to 'be like Jesus' and forgive swiftly, often this pressure causes harm... Instant forgiveness and 'putting it behind you' only delays the healing process, a journey that only begins by stating the awfulness of the violation. By shoving the story under the rug for the sake of your family or church community, you may save the perpetrator's reputation and the reputation of those near him or her, but you lose important ground in becoming free."

There is victory in loss. There is a beautiful path to walk on through the valley. With the help of the following chapters, I hope you can find it and walk it with me.

CHAPTER 2

Losing our church

"I leave the gift of peace with you—my peace. Not the kind of fragile peace given by the world, but my perfect peace. Don't yield to fear or be troubled in your hearts— instead, be courageous!" John 14:27 TPT

My husband and I started a church with another couple, in the early days of our ministry. We knew that God had spoken to us and had anointed us to take on this task. Don had a career, and I was a full-time mother of three sons. Our beginnings were small but glorious, filled with all the excitement, anticipation, fear, faith, and hope any such endeavor contains. We became wonderfully knit together with the other pastor and his wife as we served the people, and it seemed that God was blessing, rewarding, and prospering our little church. After the first couple of years, God gave us some warnings about the ways the enemy might try to come in and destroy this little work. But things were so good that we laid aside the warning. We were all quite sure that nothing like that could happen to us. We had many respected Christian leaders from around the nation who had come to our church and given prophetic words concerning our future and the place that we had in the community. God had also spoken to us as individuals, and we were confident and excited about the future.

We were growing and had all the signs of being a viable force for God in our day. After three years, my husband left his career of fourteen years to pursue full-time ministry with our church. This, again, was done after much prayer and seeking the counsel of other respected men and women of God. However, within six months, the church was destroyed from within as the couple we were co-pastoring with turned against us. Some of our best friends in the church deserted us. Untrue things were said about us. We sought help from our friends and other leaders, but all to no avail. At last, in an effort to keep from splitting the church, we simply announced we were leaving to pursue other things God was speaking to us about. This was only partially true, since we thought we were already doing what God had told us to do. However, in the best interest of the people, we felt we must do this.

Rather than keeping the church together, it split. We had lived for six months on less than one third the income we had previously depended on, but we were accused of taking extra money from the church. We had actually been living with empty cupboards and paying the church's bills before our own. So when we left the church, we had absolutely nothing to fall back on. My husband could not return to his previous job, and the economy in the city we lived in was depressed. There were no jobs to be had, and in addition to our three sons, we had two foster daughters. There were seven of us living by faith.

We were as depressed as the economy was. We had pages and pages of prophetic words, promises and Scriptures, but an empty life that only seemed to mock everything we had on paper. We felt that we must be really big losers—so much so that God couldn't trust us with His vision, so He took it away from us. We had made mistakes and knew that our mistakes had affected others, but we could not find anything we had done that would deserve this result. No church, no vision, no money! We had wonderful, faithful friends who stayed with us through this time, but they could not restore our dead vision or explain what had happened any more than we could. We could only console one another and try to go on to gain new faith and vision. Actually, what we wanted to do was quit and never go to church again! But we didn't follow that particular thought for long.

God was faithful in providing for us, doing those things only He can do: like when you open your refrigerator and all that's there is butter and some bread. Then, someone knocks on your door bringing you a grocery bag full of meat, just because God told them to (and they did not know about our situation). My husband found various odd jobs and, at last, a new job in another city. But even moving produced more loss. Because of the economy, we had to sell our home for what we owed on it, losing all we had put into it. We also had to sell two cars and many other possessions just to survive. We felt fortunate to leave town with our clothing! So, we moved and started over.

What we wanted to do was quit and never go to church again! But we didn't follow that particular thought for long.

The situation had a very negative effect on our sons. Two of them were teenagers at the time, and no matter how we tried to put a positive spin on things, they came away filled with distrust for spiritual authority. They too had lost friends and vision while seeing the pain and confusion in us. The church, under the leadership of the other pastor, fell completely apart within six months, and he moved away, taking thousands of dollars of the church's money with him. We were reconciled with many of the people from the church, even after we moved away, as everyone saw that the accusations against us had been untrue. Even the other pastor came to us to reconcile and acknowledged that the things said about us were not true.

This gave us a level of redemption that made us feel a little better. But the pain was still extreme, and some of the Christian leaders we knew were less than realistic in their assessment of how we should have handled losing. They thought we just needed to "forget it" and move on. They did not consider that shipwreck inside of us or the healing and restoration that was required. There is a time to get over it, but healing comes first. We needed time for that. We didn't really even want to hear anything from God about a ministry or serving in church—we just wanted to attend.

That didn't happen.

We had to trust God when our previous vision seemed to have been swept away in a tide of greed and not replaced. We knew the same Scriptures that every good, faithful, Bible-believing Christian quotes: God replaces ten-fold all that the enemy steals from you; all things work together for good (even though they had not, in our opinion); and on and on. Is the Word true? Will God restore ten-fold? We learned that He would—but not in the way we envisioned it. Our trust had to be in Him, and our victory was not dependent upon what we experienced outwardly. God was more interested in our insides than our outsides. He provided for us and gave us back ministry, but it didn't look the way our vision had looked in our heads and hearts.

Our trust had to be in Him, and our victory was not dependent upon what we experienced outwardly. God was more interested in our insides than our outsides.

Those sound like elementary lessons in Christianity, and they are, until you have to apply them to your own life: to the loss of your church, your ministry, your vision, and the prophetic word that has been confirmed dozens of times. They are elementary lessons until those losses appear to be permanent. Then, since your life was built around them, you have to start over with nothing. Your entire family is wounded, and you don't really know how to find healing.

CHAPTER 3

What Did We Do Wrong?

"Unless the Lord had been my help, my soul would have soon settled in silence. If I say, 'My foot slips,' Your mercy, O Lord will hold me up. In the multitude of my anxieties within me, Your comforts delight my soul." (Psalm 94:17-19, NKJV)

S elf-examination; crying; introspection; self-condemnation; questioning; a multitude of anxieties within us—that was what filled us. And always the question, "What did we do wrong?" "What is wrong with us?" His mercies did delight our souls, but there was still a multitude of anxieties within.

The Psalmist did not say that God condemned him for those "anxieties within." Instead, God listened as David poured out his soul. God gave him a season to grieve, a season for healing and pouring out his miseries. As I said in the last chapter, one church leader told us just to "forget it." His words were no comfort—and, more to the point, they were wrong. The solution to our struggle did not lie in just forgetting it, in pretending it didn't matter, or in spouting Scriptures presumptuously. The solution was in trust—trust in God, not man.

> *"Now no chastening seems to be joyful for the present, but painful; nevertheless, afterward it yields the peaceful fruit of righteousness to those who have been trained by it." (Hebrews 12:11, NKJV, emphasis mine)*

We were in the pain of God's training. What does it mean to be trained? The Oxford Dictionary defines it this way: "To teach (a person or animal) a particular skill or type of behavior through sustained practice and instruction." Whenever God's training is active in our lives, we come out more like Christ if we humble ourselves before Him. We are pruned and humbled through that time of suffering and discipline. Do we like it? Usually not—at least in the beginning.

Matthew Henry's commentary on Hebrews 12:11 puts it into a wonderful context:

*"But the Father of our souls never willingly grieves nor afflicts His children. It is always for our profit. Our whole life here is a state of childhood, and imperfect as to spiritual things; therefore, we must submit to the discipline of such a state. When we come to a perfect state, we shall be fully reconciled to all God's chastisement of us now. God's correction is not condemnation; the chastening may be borne with patience, and greatly promote holiness. **Let us then consider the afflictions brought on us by the malice of men, as corrections sent by our wise and gracious Father, for our spiritual good.**"* (emphasis mine)

Well, to be honest, it didn't feel spiritual or good. Possibly because we were short-sighted; only seeing the "now"; impatient; wanting everything to quit hurting immediately. That is what it is to be human, and God knows that we are but dust. He is tender and patient with our weakness and limitation.

At the time, we had no idea of the wonderful things God could bring for us out of the pain. The afflictions we were enduring were not brought on by God; however, we wondered why an omnipotent God let this happen. Why did He tell us one thing and seemingly do another? We had a great deal to learn about God's ways and methods being higher than ours. When you are in pain, it can be hard to remember that. When I am hurt by someone, I want to blame them. I do blame them! It's easy to blame God as well.

Can you question God and still be a leader in the church? Of course. Listen to David in Psalm 11:1-2, *"How long O Eternal One? How long will you forget Me? Forever? How long will You look the other way? How long must I agonize, grieving your absence in my heart everyday? How long will you let my enemies win?"* (The Voice) Can you blame a person and still be an elder in the church? Yes. Even though the fight is not against flesh and blood, it *was* flesh and blood—the malice of men—that had nearly destroyed us spiritually and financially. It left a deep imprint of distrust on the hearts of our children, no matter how much we tried to wipe it away with the Word. In order to be victorious in loss, we had to accept that injustice had happened, and that God would redeem it for us. God wasn't trying to kill us—He wanted to transform our pain, teach us valuable lessons that hold their truth for eternity.

We were eventually able to forgive the other pastor. Forgiveness and the end of pain are not simultaneous; the second follows the first at a distance not determined by the level of your faith. Rather, it is determined ultimately by the unfailing love God has for you, a love that will carry you through your worst pain and piece you back together again, in time.

*"It is good for me that I have been afflicted, that I may learn Your statutes... Unless Your law had been my delight, I would have perished in my affliction. I will never forget Your precepts **for by them You have given me life**." (Psalm 119:71, 93, NKJV, emphasis mine)*

Forgiveness and the end of pain are not simultaneous; the second follows the first at a distance not determined by the level of your faith.

I am thankful that, unlike David, we do not have to measure up to the old law any longer. But we still have to learn His precepts—they give us His life. When you are in a leadership position in church or you are a staff pastor, it can be quite difficult to put this in perspective. One day, all the people see you preaching, praying, ministering, leading; and then, the next day, they see you sitting on a chair at home. The assumptions, silent accusations, and appearance of failure can be overwhelming. You feel as though you may perish in your affliction. What do you say to the flock who once looked to you as their shepherd?

What do you say to other pastors whose churches are flourishing, when yours has just crashed and burned? How do you answer the silent thoughts you believe are going through their minds—because they are going through yours?

At that time in our own lives, the belief about any failure was that you failed because you must have sinned. You must have done something very wrong, or this would not have happened. A simple theology: if you're doing everything right, nothing wrong will happen. Just not a true one.

The Christian formula we had learned was to mix faith with the Word, stir in a lot of positive confession, add some Bible college and determination, and you will succeed. If there is failure, it is your fault, because you must have missed one of the steps. If another pastor turns against you, then you stand in front of the mirror wondering what unseen sin is lurking there that turned you from God's chosen to God's reject. All the while, you tell yourself that none of these things are true, but you suffer under the knowledge that this may be what some Christians are thinking. Sometimes Christians deal with their wounded by simply finishing them off using the sword of the Word to cut their hearts out rather than pouring in the healing, anointing oil of the Spirit. It is so easy to judge the lives of others, supplying them with edicts of what they should have done. Many of the judgments we so freely send out on others in their time of desperation may return back to us, for in the same way you judge, you will be judged: what a fearful thing.

"With my soul I have desired You in the night, yes, by my spirit within me I will seek You early; for when your judgments are in the earth, the inhabitants of the world will learn righteousness." (Isaiah 26:9, NKJV)

Judgment: decision, determination, judgment; a personal cause or right; justice, rectification, correction, punishment. Judgment is that faculty (always found in God, and **sometimes** in man) that produces decisions based on justice, rightness, truth, fairness, and equity. Judgment rectifies imbalance and sets things right again. God's judgments are always true and correct. Ours? Not so much.

I see judgment like a red light at an intersection. It is not there to punish or cause harm to anyone. It exists for the opposite purpose: safety and order. It is a tool to "set things right." If I run the light and get a ticket, I bring a judgment down on myself. If I run a red light and hit another car, an innocent person is harmed because of my failure. They are not being judged; I am, and the Judge won't let me blame the red light.

What if I'm the innocent party? I didn't do anything wrong, but I got hurt anyway. The light isn't at fault. I will definitely be angry with the other person, and I may suffer greatly because of what they did. The law and the red light were meant to prevent my harm, but I am innocent and hurt anyway. In the same way, we were innocent yet hurt by the actions of another person. God never intended that humanity would lie and cheat and hurt one another. He established the law of love because He is love. Jesus said we should be known by our love for one another, but, sometimes, a church or a person is a car wreck. It is not God who hurts the people—it is people hurting people. People breaking God's law of love and servanthood.

What happened in our church was not a "judgment" on us. It was a result of someone else running a red light. It was never, ever what God wanted. However, because of a wonderful thing called free will, people can hurt one another. Once it happens—once the car is wrecked—the guilty and the innocent have to live with the consequences and try to put their lives back together.

We live with natural laws like gravity. If I let go of something, it will fall. If it is delicate, it will break. If I throw something, it will move through the air and may hurt whatever it hits. God did not break up our church, destroy our vision, or hurt us. He did not make accusations against us. He did not turn against us. He did not reach out and hurt the hearts of the people in our church. He does not reach down and "judge" us by wreaking havoc in our lives. God does not cause car wrecks or drop our delicate lives and break them. People do it by breaking the law of love—running the red light, throwing your heart against a wall. It is the injustice of man against man.

Why doesn't God stop it? Again—the greatest honor and trust God gave to humanity was free will. He wanted us to love and serve Him out of our free will, not because we were forced to. It became a double-edged sword. Once humanity entered into sin, it meant that free will could be used for good or evil. God does intervene: one-by-one, personally, lovingly, patiently. He trains, heals, teaches, and guides us. Time. He allows us time. He *uses* time. It is His. As we keep our eyes on Him and heart open to Him, He brings us through. Even when our eyes are so full of tears we cannot see, and our hearts so wounded we cannot muster any faith, still He cares for us and is working on our behalf. He will restore. He will shower love upon us. As we grow, we learn how to deal with the injustice of a fallen life and to find God's path through it.

There are times when you may be caught in something greater than yourself. That is very hard to accept, because our culture is all about self-determination, freedom, and free will. In the kingdom of God, we learn that this is only half of the picture. In God's kingdom, both the community *and* the individual matter, and God will care for both. Judgment is not always a bad thing. Things need to be set right. You might be in the middle of the rectifying of an imbalance in a friend, a neighbor, a family, a church, a city, or a nation. There will be what looks like personal injustice associated with it. In situations like this, it can bring unexpected comfort to take our eyes off our personal good and see the greater picture. Then we can rest in knowing that our loss, though personally unjust, is not only about us. You may have to endure a trial that was not brought on by anything you did, but you may still lose something.

Pastors believe in and teach on the death and resurrection of a vision. Sometimes visions must go through the process of death and then rebirth, as the Spirit of God breathes new life on them, bringing them to pass again. Pastors believe in the fact that, if a ministry is somehow lost, God will restore it. We believe in the fulfillment of the prophetic word. All of these things are true. However, there are also those times when one vision dies and stays dead—at least, in the form it first took. Does that mean that the vision was not of God and that is why it had to die? No. If your ministry is temporarily offline, it does not mean you heard God incorrectly, and because of your mistake, God took it from you. If a prophetic word comes and is confirmed, and seems to be coming to fulfillment, yet is blown away like dust, God is still the one who spoke it. It does not mean that God was only kidding. It is not a cruel joke He played just to see how we would respond. He loves us and only does that which is for our good; but it may not feel good at the time. It sure didn't for us. Little did we know what the future would bring us.

You may be part of a corporate vision that dies, and, since your vision is tied to that larger picture, your vision seems to die too. God's vision will rise again, but it may not be in a form that looks like what you think it should. God is always trying to get us to see beyond ourselves: to see through His eyes. If your vision was connected to a place or time where a wreck happened, your vision may appear to die. It really doesn't—it may just be offline for a while—but God's word is always true. He will continue that work in you.

For us, God dealt with not only us, but some much greater injustices and wrongs that were taking place in our church and the people, including us. God moved us out of the way, actually sparing us even greater pain. We could not see that at the time. It is sometimes hard to see through the veil of pain, rejection, and loss. Even later, it was still hard to see because of the lingering pain. God didn't mind! He loved us through it. Time: it is a gift.

Our society deals with pain in a hundred different, non-biblical ways. We reject it; we blame it on someone; we judge ourselves and others by it; we see it as only negative. In America, pain does not happen to the truly good and gifted (we are told). We may make a few exceptions, but overall, we are all supposed to look like actors and actresses and live like millionaires. The only other acceptable thing is to live at the other end of the spectrum: to be totally odd and out there. Christians have been eager to accept the health and wealth dialogue (which only works in America), and usually works the best for the person preaching the message. I haven't seen or heard of any Christians in developing nations who have been able to name and claim a million dollars and a new Lexus. They are often not even able to find a meal. They are experiencing many types of pain. Yet they will walk for miles and miles to hear more about Jesus while we Americans can barely get out of bed to drive five miles to church.

This isn't a condemnation of anyone; it is simply a symptomatic by-product of our society. All societies have their own unique blind spots. In American, one of our blinds spots is the truth that pain is part of the kingdom. Just as we need to learn about handling injustice, we must also learn how to find the beauty within and through pain. If you keep looking, you will see it.

Where do you look? Straight at Jesus—the author and finisher of your faith!

Perseverance in trials and correction really does produce the peaceful fruit of righteousness. There is a place in God of learning to trust—not in the fulfillment of promises and prophecies; not the resurrection of a vision—but to hope in Him only, not just in what He does. In that place of processing injustice, we find that He alone knows what true justice is. True justice is not what I think it is because, for each of us, our justice means that we get our way and our suffering ends. But God sees justice from an eternal perspective. He sees justice through the eyes of many, as well as through the eyes of the one. Facing injustice in this life and trusting in this way does not mean you have given up or become passive.

It does not mean you have put faith aside. It does mean you have learned simple, childlike faith and obedience, and your faith is in God, not in your own idea of the way things ought to be. You may even be right, but God is more right. It means that your faith is so strong it does not depend on outward, visible manifestation. You have learned to trust the unseen and the One who rules there.

Victory.

CHAPTER 4

Hebrews 11

"Yet indeed I also count all things loss for the excellence of the knowledge of Christ Jesus my Lord, for whom I have suffered the loss of all things, and count them as rubbish, that I may gain Christ and be found in Him, not having my own righteousness which is from the law, but that which is through faith in Christ, the righteousness which is from God by faith; that I may know Him and the power of His resurrection, and the fellowship of His sufferings, being conformed to His death." (Philippians 3:8-10, NKJV)

t is hard to count "all things" as loss. I personally do *not* like it. However, Paul has a completely different view. He isn't looking at things; He is focused on *knowing Christ*. That's what makes all the difference.

Why wasn't Paul contending for the promises of Abraham? He was in a jail cell facing death. Why did he have such peace and acceptance of the circumstances of his life? Was he just a defeated man? It's easy for us to think that Paul was just "different from us." Maybe he was "special"; it was a different time; he was a single man, so it was easier; he knew that this was his lot in life; being a martyr is different than our kind of suffering; people in that day had different expectations.

None of those things are true. Paul was a human being with all the same emotions, passions, needs, and desires we have. He knew the promises of Abraham, but he was not demanding that God bring them to pass in front of *his* eyes. He was not asking the Philippians to agree in prayer with him that the devil would be bound and his chains would be loosed *right now*; that all the money he had lost would be restored tenfold; that they come against all the curses of man and stand in faith with him.

Furthermore, he was not regarded by anyone as a loser who didn't have the faith or power to get out of jail. Although there were times when chains fell off and people were freed, Paul was not demanding it as part of "his vision." Think of what he could have done if he had not been in jail—the converts, the healing, the writing, and the sermons. He had learned a truth of victory in losing that we must all learn: all he wanted was to "know Him in the power of His resurrection, and the fellowship of His sufferings." Few of us pray for that very often. Paul prayed this because of where his focus was. And because he was no different from us, we, too, can desire to know Christ in this way: above all else.

Hebrews 11 says that faith is the substance, the realization of things hoped for; the evidence, confidence of things not seen. Hope is not realized because I obtain what I hope for, and faith is not faith because I finally touch and experience, here on earth, what I had faith in. *Hope is realized and maintained in my growing, intimate relationship with God.*

The actualization in this life of what I hope for is wonderful, but it is not guaranteed. Faith is gained and maintained on the basis of God's Word and the knowledge that, no matter what I see or don't see, God is faithful and true. Abraham is called the Father of faith, and yet *he never saw or touched what he believed for.* Isaac was not the fulfillment of the promises Abraham had been given. He was only the beginning. Abraham was promised a city whose builder and maker was God. He was promised that his seed would be greater in number than the sand. He never saw either of those things with earthly eyes, yet he believed and hoped and never gave up.

Do you see him as a failure because he never achieved that royal city in his time here on earth? We have believed a lie—that if we do not see the actualization of what we had faith in, then we are faithless, small failures; that if what we believed in and trusted in falls and dies, we are losers. If so, then Abraham was a fraud, and God lied about him. Our faithfulness is shown in our perseverance in believing the Word and promises of God, *no matter what we see or don't see.* In this, there is rest.

One of the problems the Jewish leadership had with Jesus was this: He was not the conquering, powerful person they were looking for. The Torah contained descriptions of a King who would come and destroy the enemies of these people and set them free. In the context of their times, they were looking for a man with a sword and shield who would gather up a mighty army and bring vengeance on the Romans and everyone else who had oppressed the Jewish tribes.

When Jesus came, people called Him the King of Kings, but He didn't look like the picture they had in their minds. He looked weak. He looked vulnerable. However, a strange thing happened. He did gather an army, but it was an army of peaceful people led by unimportant fishermen, hated tax collectors, and others who held no power in government or any other area. In the eyes of the Jewish leaders, the followers themselves were common or worse.

In spite of their efforts to stop this, the strange movement grew, and Jesus threatened their power because more people followed and listened to Him than to the establishment.

This weak nobody could not possibly be the King they were waiting for! He hung out with the lowest forms of life in every city He went to. No true conquering King, sent by the all-powerful God, would look Him or act like Him. He made Himself lowly and vulnerable. That vulnerability could not exist in their conquering King. He didn't kill any of their enemies! Instead, He said ridiculous things like, "Love your enemy." And more and more people called Him King.

To the establishment, Jesus was nothing more than some vagrant who got lucky and performed a few miracles. He was an annoyance, and yet He was a threat. The word *vulnerable* means "capable of being physically or emotionally wounded; open to attack or damage." A person who was going to free all of Israel would not be vulnerable. They viewed Him as a loser. So they killed Him. Surely this would end their problems and then the *real* King could come.

That plan didn't work out very well for them. They couldn't see that Jesus had to be wounded physically and emotionally. He had to be open to attack. Father Richard Rohr, in his blog post of March 16, 2016, says this:

> *"It takes all of us a long time to move from power to weakness, from glib certitude to vulnerability, from meritocracy to the ocean of grace. Strangely enough, this is especially true for people raised in religion. In Paul's letters, he consistently idealizes not power but powerlessness, not strength but weakness, not success but the cross. It's as if*

he's saying, 'I glory when I fail and suffer because now I get to be like Jesus—the naked loser—who turned any notion of God on its head.' Now the losers can win, and, even better we are all losers!"

From here we can see the victory in learning to lose well. It goes against everything we hear or want to be true. Who wants to lose? Who wants to come in second, or worse yet, last? If the prophetic word spoken over you does not come to pass, does that mean you are a "loser"? Never! Through all that we went through in the years we spent in ministry, we learned to stay in a place of quiet strength. We learned to fight smart and how to live to fight again another day with a faith that grows stronger and stronger because it's not focused on what we see as being "right." **We learn to stop contending with flesh—our own and others**!

All that we may lose is reputation, position, or things, but we never lose who and what we are in Christ. The truth of God's Word isn't centered on me and the fulfillment of my word, vision, or life's work. It is centered on Christ and Christ alone. We need to let each other go through the pain of learning to focus on Christ: yes, the pain of learning. When my focus is on my vision, my ministry, my life, or my prophetic word, then it cannot possibly be wholly on Him, no matter how much I protest to the contrary. After all, we argue, the vision *is* Him; the ministry I have *is* Him—how could anyone say that I am not focused on God?

I have said all those things as I protested against what was happening! After we moved away from the city where our church fell, we became the worship leaders at the new church we were attending. We did find healing, and we did find our previous ministry manifested again. It looked much different, but there it was: reborn in a new form. God opened up the doors He knew needed to be opened, not the ones we necessarily wanted. We then went on to another church where we poured out our lives for many years. We were deeply blessed and hurt there.

Then—guess what we did? Because it went so well the first time, we started another church in another city! It went sort of like the first one—great, then awful, then dead. Talk about going around that mountain again. My husband was crushed. He went into a deep depression for about a year. We attended a large church and were basically invisible for a year. We needed that time to heal and find our way again.

All that I did in the past has built what I am to be now. All that I am going through now is building what I will be in the future

Then God led us to the church where I am now. We became part of the leadership team, and God gave us the people, the ministry, the love that we had always wanted. But we are not there because we finally found a church that is doing everything "right" (our way) and is filled with perfect people who never disappoint anyone. They're human, and so are we.

God gave back ministry to my husband and me, and it was more wonderful than ever before, but that cannot be where our fulfillment is. Where I am at now, God has taken all of the past and woven it in as part of the vision and ministry that is needed now. All that I did in the past has built what I am able to be now. All that I am going through right now is building what I will be in the future! It didn't come my way or in my time, and it did not resemble what I thought it would. God has brought new vision, but He did not rebirth "my" old vision just like I had seen it. I had to let Him bring something new into my life, after learning to be content with His way rather than mine. As I said, there are some areas of ministry that God has never restored, even when I tried to get them back! I had to learn to accept that as being from the hand of God not the injustice of man, even when I knew God had spoken about my involvement in a particular area of ministry. After all, there are seasons for things, and each season is different.

For so long, I had no rest in my soul, in turmoil, fighting, exhausted and confused. The Lord was with me then. And He brought me through it. At last came a time when I was able to relent, a time of rest and peace and victory. I lost, but I am not a loser. Instead, I have found a place of bright victory. I am not doing the things I did before, but I am happy and content with what I am doing: helping others. After all, that's what it is all about: loving and serving others. God did restore things to me; I have a beautiful home, the most amazing family, and wonderful and faithful friends. I am at peace in the midst of great personal loss. I have changed and will never be the person I was. Hopefully, I will be closer and closer to the image of Christ every day.

Our sons have learned to trust in God and not humanity and to trust God to work through others for their good. We believe even more strongly in the promises of God, in their fulfillment in our lives and the lives of others, because our faith does not depend upon them being done our way. We fight all the more diligently against the wiles of the enemy, because victory is not evidenced in our lives alone, but in the life of Christ and His bride, the church. We are not striving just to apprehend a vision or a prophecy; we are running in such a way as to win the ultimate prize—Jesus Christ. The evidence of my victory is in how much I am conformed to His image, not how many prophecies have been fulfilled in my life. Now that is victory, no matter how much I had to lose to obtain it!

I am at peace in the midst of great personal loss.

CHAPTER 5

Living In Christ

"My old identity has been co-crucified with Messiah and no longer lives; for the nails of his cross crucified me with him. And now the essence of this new life is no longer mine, for the Anointed One lives his life through me—we live in union as one! My new life is empowered by the faith of the Son of God who loves me so much that he gave himself for me, and dispenses his life into mine!" Galatians 2:20 TPT

If you—a minister or a servant—have lost a ministry, a position, or a vision, you are not a loser. If you know someone who has gone through those losses, do not regard them as a loser. If you have sinned, repent and move forward in forgiveness, learning as you go. If you have suffered injustice, you are in the company of Christ, who suffered the ultimate injustice.

There really is such a thing as being a loser who won. Loss does not walk hand-in-hand with being a failure. While you are in the midst of learning how to handle the injustice, readjusting to a life without the old vision, focusing on Christ alone and putting past prophecy to rest in His hands, there is a place of peace, healing, and restoration. God gave the first prophetic word. God brought you through the death of that word. And now, God is speaking a new word. The revealing of the Word will look the way God wants it to look, and quite often it is not at all the way we see it or try to make it look. He doesn't condemn us for trying to make a vision look a certain way! He applauds our efforts, just as we applaud the efforts of our children as we gently redirect them where needed. Sometimes, though, we build something that has to be renovated by Him to look the way He knows it really should look, and it's for our good.

You may have received a prophetic word about being a "leader" in the body of Christ, yet you are stuck back in the nursery. You may love babies, but— come on—this is *not* what you saw as the fulfillment of that prophecy. Maybe it is, maybe it isn't. Maybe it is the preparation of becoming a servant to "the least of these" in the eyes of society (in God's eyes, we know babies are not "least"). Maybe it's a stepping stone toward the leadership He has in mind for you in the future. Maybe the fulfillment of that prophecy is years away, and you just need to remain faithful! It may not look very glorious in our eyes, but in God's eyes, it is wonderful. The fulfillment requires humility, a willingness to submit to God's way of doing things and God's timing. It's His church, not ours. It's His will, not mine. He is the creator of all things; I copy His creation as I focus on being conformed to His image.

God allows us to go through painful times, and He gives us the space and provision we need, as we look to Him as our all in all. Whatever is lost will be replaced—just let Him determine how, when, and what it will look like. And if it's not what you thought it would be, learn to laugh and trust, because one day, all that will matter is that you are found in Him. In these days, God is taking our eyes and turning them outward to see a world in which there are more important issues than whether or not our ministry looks like we think it should—a world where there are more important judgments to make than whether or not another pastor had enough faith. Is it more important that the pastor recognizes my great gift as a worship leader (and puts me up on the platform), or that I'm missing an opportunity to reach out in love to my neighbor because I spend more time praying for myself than for him?

Our ministry is the sum of who we are in Christ.

God, give us Your vision—it is greater than ourselves. Whatever our disappointments may be, the one lesson we must learn is that we are not the sum of our ministry—our ministry is the sum of who we are in Christ. The widow who gave her mite in an offering plate has had more sermons preached about her than many pastors and lay pastors who strove so diligently to preach and teach, to believe and prove that the Word of God was true. She silently demonstrated her faith with a penny put in an offering plate, and her life is commemorated throughout the ages in the most famous Book ever. She thought nothing of reputation or ministry, but it came to her through a selfless, simple act of obedience in which she laid her whole life in God's hand. And she probably never knew that Jesus made her a lesson for the ages!

Although my reputation is important and is most often a proof of who and what I am, it is still not the ultimate proof. If the loss of my reputation causes me to give up, then I am not what I claimed to be. A lost reputation can be reclaimed. God is in the business of exposing lies and bringing truth out from under the heaviest load of accusation. I am what I claimed to be if I persevere and continue to stand, trusting God, maintaining the same life of integrity privately that I lived publicly, before my reputation was slandered. The evidence of my faith is not my reputation, my ministry, or my position. The evidence of my faith was made manifest two thousand years ago as God became man and victoriously lost His life, then regained it as the forerunner for all humanity. My position in ministry is not the proof of my being called, anointed, and blessed by God.

In 1 Samuel 16:14-16, Saul, the King of Israel, maintained his position even after the Spirit and anointing had departed. The position proved nothing, but we often tie our egos and worth to position—until it is taken from us so that God can show us that the proof of our calling is in the fact that He said we were called, not in our position in a church or organization. I may lose the position, but I do not lose the call or anointing unless I choose to turn away from God and deny the Holy Spirit. It's alright to go through loss and take time to let the pain heal, to forgive, and to find freedom, dignity, and victory in losing. It's alright to hurt and then to move forward. It's alright to lose.

When we see two championship teams play against each other for the prize, and the "loser" leaves the court crying and disappointed, we quickly forget it. We focus on the smiling winner—everyone loves a winner. The minute the game is over, however, the coach of the losing team begins strategizing for the next year and how to get there again to win. But in the church, when we see a potential champion go down in defeat, we sometimes blame them and allow them to berate themselves. Where is the coach who will help them start planning their comeback? The best coach is one who has experienced loss. We need coaches like that in the church. They will coach with compassion and truth, because they know about the victory that lies on the other side of defeat.

You will come back. Not because of your greatness that was stripped away, but because of His greatness. My desire is to be one of those coaches who helps others and comforts them with the same comfort with which I was comforted. We need more coaches. Funny thing about coaches—they are on the sidelines. The public doesn't see all their hard work, all the hours spent watching their players; watching videos of their team and other teams; agonizing over how to get their team to the finish line. If they are really good, we may see them on television, but the star will be the quarterback or some other player. The coach will be acknowledged, but if they have a losing season, the coach may be fired. The players stay; the coach is out. He or she is still a coach. They are no less talented than the year that they won.

Because of your experience of loss in ministry, you are best qualified to help others. If you have not yet experienced loss, you will. That is not a negative confession; it is simply an acknowledgment that we live in a broken world. Yet despite that, God can turn our loss into gain. The best lessons I have learned as a Christian have come out of loss. The greatest victory I have found has come as I lost. The greatest defeat to the enemy has come out of loss, because it was then that Christ rose as the champion, and no enemy can stand against Him. Vision, reputation, ministry, and every promise are all under His wing.

There are areas of ministry that I participated in for years and years. I was a worship leader in small groups and churches. I'm no longer in that position, yet I have the blessing of knowing that it was a wonderful part of my life. The Word says there is a time for everything. It also makes it clear that the time for some things comes to an end!

Today, I am in a different time of life, and I could interpret that to mean that a "ministry" died, or that I am being denied that ministry. But there is another perspective I can take: God's perspective. All that happened was that the time for me to do that is now over. In this new life I am learning to live, I have other ministries. I loved leading worship! It was wonderful. I love to worship in my car, in my house, at work (if I can), and anywhere I happen to be. One of the greatest times of worship I have is on my motorcycle. It is glorious, like heaven is all around me. But that's definitely not the same as being a worship leader up on the platform. Yet the desire to be "standing in the synagogues and on street corners to be seen by men" (Matthew 6) needs to die in me, so that I may gain Christ.

Maybe you were the head pastor of a church. Maybe you led missions teams and saw great salvations and miracles. Maybe you taught and did a fantastic job, and people loved your teaching.

Maybe the time for that has come to an end. Maybe it will come again, but be all different than before. The missions trips to faraway lands may be replaced by sitting with your neighbor in your living room and leading them to Christ. The same, yet different.

CHAPTER 6

Separation and Reconciliation

U ntil this point, we have spoken mostly of injustice: when betrayal or wrong lead to the death of a vision. Sometimes our loss is not a result of human injustice, however; death, grief, sickness, or chronic pain also come into our lives and leave us broken-hearted.

When my husband died, I had a very vivid picture of separation. It was as if I had stepped through an invisible wall into a life that was running parallel to my life, and I was trapped there. I could not go back. I saw my happy, wonderful past life on the other side, so close that surely I could reach out and touch it—but no. I was trapped in this parallel world of horror, separation, loneliness, and pain. The separation seemed unbearable, in part because it was irreversible. I could never go back.

Some separation is bearable. If you are temporarily separated from someone, you can stand it, because there is a point in the future where you will be together again. Other separation is permanent: death. Death of a person—death of your reputation—death of a ministry—death of a vision.

The absolute inability to change what has happened; knowing you can never get back to that place where you were; losing that which defined your life; these bitter truths are your companions behind that devastating, transparent wall.

At first, you spend your time looking through the wall at what you had. You look back because there is no forward—at least, no forward that you want to see. Going forward would mean going on without all that is on the other side. You can't go back. You don't want to go forward. You feel trapped in a hell of pain, loss, and permanent separation.

Accepting permanent separation from someone or something you loved and gave your life to is such an anguishing transition. I did not want to stop looking at the life I had, because looking away would mean that it was really gone. Somehow, if I could just keep looking, maybe I could find a way back. I knew I couldn't, but it was all I wanted. The moment-by-moment forward flow of life called me, even though I didn't want anything that I saw ahead of me. All I had wanted was just a step behind me through that wall—a place I could never go to again.

I think that all permanent loss is that way. As Christians, we have hope—hope in Him. We have the Holy Spirit, the Comforter, at work within our hearts and souls. When friends desert you, your vision dies, your ministry is lost, your life is devastated—there is a God who cares, sees, knows, hears, and on whose wings we may be carried forward.

Great loss produces great grief. Grief is all about loss: all different types of loss. In my own season of grief, I read lots of books on the subject—even threw one in the trash whose author said they just "floated" through grief.

I was not floating. I was on the floor sobbing, trying to dig my way under that wall back to the life that had been torn away from me. I cried, screamed, had a full-blown pity party, hid under a blanket.

But one thing I knew for sure: in the darkest part of the Valley, there was still a light shining. At first, I didn't want to look at it, but the more I did, the better it was. Little by little, moment by moment, each tiny step brought me closer to the light as it grew. I prayed—looked up, looked back, looked forward—and prayed, prayed, prayed.

Somewhere along the path, the wall disappears, and the two paths forward merge together into a changed life. Both the path and the one walking it have changed incalculably. The light is full again, and you can finally look ahead to see the future God has waiting for you.

> Somewhere along the path, the wall disappears, and the two paths forward merge together into a changed life. Both the path and the one walking it have changed incalculably.

We never know how long this journey to that changed life will take, because there is no timer at the beginning of the Valley. Your journey through it is not a race; disregard anyone who tries to time you. And the Valley is also not a place to build a house and live in. Pitch a tent, but don't build a house.

Part of God's work in you during the Valley journey is to merge what *was* with what *is* to produce what *will be*. He takes what was lost and grafts it into what is to come. It is a painful, yet beautiful, process. It is reconciliation, a reuniting. It is what Jesus came to do—reconcile us back to the Father. He brought us together again. He tore down the agonizing wall of separation and made us one with the Father again through His blood. The heavenly example is the natural example for our journey. In the Garden, Jesus asked for this cup of separation to be taken from Him:

Then He took Peter and the two sons of Zebedee with Him, and He grew sorrowful and deeply distressed.

Jesus: *My soul is overwhelmed with grief, to the point of death. Stay here and keep watch with Me.*

He walked a little farther and finally fell prostrate and prayed.

Jesus: *Father, this is the last thing I want. If there is any way, please take this bitter cup from Me. Not My will, but Yours be done. (Matthew 26:37-39, The Voice)*

The result was new life for all who believed. That's all He asks: believe in Him, and He will transform you.

Jesus didn't stay in the Garden. He moved through death into life. Throughout this temporary journey on earth—we do the same.

And so it is: God transforms our loss into the most incredible win!

And so it is: God transforms our loss into the most incredible win!

About the Author

Fleda Bennie - author, wife, mother, grandmother, friend, minister, entrepreneur. and motorcycle rider - has been involved in Christian ministry since she was twenty-four. With exposure to many wonderful teachers, pastors, friends and experiences, she lives with a heart to see others built up, encouraged, informed and walking in the truth, joy, hope and peace that comes only from a relationship with Christ. After all the years of listening, observing and learning life's lessons, she is sharing her experiences with the hope of helping others who might be living through similar circumstances. Having pastored, preached, taught, written, and worked in multiple ministries in and out of the church, her heart is extended to those who are also serving in the Christian community. Being a Christian and serving is a tremendously rewarding adventure. However, as with all aspects of life, there can be pain, disappointment and disillusionment along the way. Her goal is to learn and grow through each hard spot, and then move ever deeper into the fantastic adventure of walking with Jesus.

You can find her at WomenMinistering.com.

Made in United States
Troutdale, OR
06/29/2023

10874333R00039

Made in the USA
Las Vegas, NV
01 November 2024

10686069R00111